Origin and History

Birds are bipeds, and covered with feathers. No other Earth creature has this type of covering. Nearly all birds have the power of flight. The feathers, which serve as clothing, also assist in flying, protect from heat and cold and create their beauty.

The earliest traces of existence of birds in the world are supposed to be bird tracks found in sandstone in the Connecticut Valley. Fossil birds have been found in New Jersey, Kansas and Idaho. A fossil bird with teeth has been found in Kansas. An

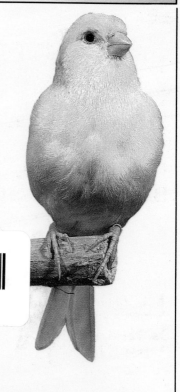

A Yellow Buff Border Fancy Canary. The Border Fancy Canary comes in a variety of colors, but the yellow has always been the most popular. ▶

extinct bird of New Zealand has been found in fossil deposits; it had legs and feet nearly as massive as those of an elephant. Skeletons of some of these birds may be seen at the Museum of Natural History in New York.

The Canary was native to the Canary Islands and was a small grayish-green bird. History tells us that in the Sixteenth Century sailors trapped many of these birds to take home to Italy. The sailors were shipwrecked near the island of Elba, but finally some of these birds reached Italy. They immediately became popular and from there spread all over the world.

All the varieties of Canaries we know today have been developed from these little green birds.

Border Fancy Canary. The Border Fancy Canary is by far the most popular variety of canary. This is largely due to its elegant and dainty appearance as well as its fine song. ◀

There are many different T.F.H. books available on canaries, all available at your local pet store. ◀

Desirability of Birds in the Home

Birds have been regarded for centuries as one of the most delightful creatures of nature, and no music is sweeter than the beautiful song of a Canary in your home. The warm color of their plumage, their graceful motions, their peculiar habits and manners as well as their song, all possess a charm that wins the most indifferent. They win the hearts of all who love beauty, grace and sweetness. Years ago Wordsworth wrote:

The birds around me hopped and played,
Their thoughts I cannot measure;
But the least motion which they made
It seemed a thrill of pleasure.

A dark, dreary house seems to come alive when a Canary begins to sing. A palace becomes a home when a Canary becomes one of its occupants.

A Canary is a wonderful companion for elderly people. If they are lonely it brings them companionship. It gives them something to love and to love them in return. It gives them responsibility in caring for the bird, something, perhaps, they have been missing since their family had grown and no longer needed them. I have known people with nervous breakdowns or imaginary ills who became interested in Canaries and forgot their troubles. One lady

A Red-factor Canary. The Red-factor Canary came about from a cross breeding of a wild canary to a Red Hooded Siskin Finch. The red coloring of the finch became a part of the canary's genetic make-up. ☚

Yorkshire Canary. The Yorkshire Canary is typically known for its large size. It can attain a length of 18-20 cm.(7-8 in.). ▶

Variegated Yorkshire Canary. The most common colors of the Yorkshire Canary are Yellow and White birds and some with slight markings. ☚

told me that she had been going to the doctor several times a week when she became interested in Canaries. She said that after that she forgot to go to the doctor; in fact she didn't need to anymore!

Children are always interested in birds and a Canary in their home becomes one of the family. When they can share in care of the bird it teaches them dependability and reliability.

I have heard folks say that they didn't like to see a bird in a cage. If the cage is right and their needs are properly taken care of, they are happy. They have been born and bred in captivity for centuries and could not live free in nature any longer.

For very detailed information about everything you always wanted to know about canaries, but did not know where to look; T.F.H. Publications offers a variety of specialized books that will supply everything you are looking for. ◂

◂ Yellow American Singer. The American Singer is the only breed of canary that has been cultivated in the United States. Most other varieties of canaries originated in England or Germany.

Frosted Canary. When the plumage of a canary appears to have whitish edges, it is called "frosted". ▸

Frosted Red-factor Canary. The frosting of this Red-factor canary somewhat diminishes the intensity of its coloring. ◆

Yorkshire Canary crossbred with a Scotch Fancy. Canaries are often crossbred to other varieties to improve upon color, size, or song. ▶

Frosted Red-factor. Frosting of a canary is often referred to as non-intensive because of the lack of color at the ends of the feathers. ◆

General Care

SELECTION

There are various kinds of Canaries from which you can choose. One's own wishes and likes should be the deciding factor in deciding which variety of bird should become a new member of one's family.

If you like color and a good all-around song then the color bred Canary is the best and the most available in pet shops all over the country. If you

are more interested in a low pitched, beautifully toned singer, then the Roller Canary should be chosen. These are usually readily available in most pet shops. If one wishes something different and out of the usual, one of the type birds should be investigated. Not many pet shops keep these birds, but your pet dealer can probably procure them for you if you make your wishes known to him.

When selecting a bird pick a young one that looks in good condition. Feathers should be clean and well groomed. He should be alert and eyes should be bright. A bird who sits with his feathers drooped, perhaps with his head under his wing in the daytime, is not a well bird and will only bring you grief.

Perhaps I should mention that only male birds in the Canary world make good singers. Occasionally a female bird will sing a little but not a continuing, connected song.

Only an experienced bird handler can tell by sight what the sex of a Canary is. Generally the male is more bold, and his song is sweet and has a ring to it. Compared to that of the male, the song of the female is like a warble, if she sings at all. Also, the female does not hold herself up as the male does.

If you want a male Canary it is best to buy only from a reliable pet dealer. Canary breeders will sometimes try to sell extra females as males to unwary customers.

A reliable pet dealer will give you a written guarantee that the Canary is a male. The guarantee should also state in writing that the bird will sing and that if the bird does not sing the purchaser can return the bird for a refund. The time limit for singing is usually fourteen days.

The pet dealer will stamp the wings of the bird with indelible ink. This is for his protection, to insure that if the bird is returned it is the same one he has guaranteed. The ink will fade within a month when the bird sheds. Naturally, with all these precautions male Canaries cost considerably more than the females.

In a clean, well kept pet shop the attendant can

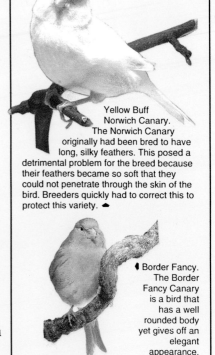

Yellow Buff Norwich Canary. The Norwich Canary originally had been bred to have long, silky feathers. This posed a detrimental problem for the breed because their feathers became so soft that they could not penetrate through the skin of the bird. Breeders quickly had to correct this to protect this variety. ◆

◀ Border Fancy. The Border Fancy Canary is a bird that has a well rounded body yet gives off an elegant appearance.

White Canary and Blue Canary. Coloring of canaries has changed dramatically from the wild green coloration that, at one time, was the only thing in existence. ◆

Yellow Border Fancy. The Border Fancy Canary appreciates all types of toys within its cage to occupy its time. ◄

Red-factor Canary. Canaries make excellent pets for children. The color of the bird is only a matter of personal preference. ▶

Frosted Red-factor. Frosting was once not desired by birdkeepers because it was believed to take away from the beauty of the bird. Now, frosting is widely accepted by bird fanciers all over the world. ◄

be of great help in making your selection. He will become acquainted with the alert, good singing bird and can give you good advice.

METABOLISM

Canaries have a much faster metabolism than human beings and other mammals. For instance,

the human heart beats 70 to 80 times a minute, but a Canary's heart beats 800 to 1,000 times a minute. Holding a Canary in your hand is like holding a small motor: you can feel the heart beating rapidly. Canaries do not have pores to regulate temperature and cannot sweat. They cool themselves by breathing with their mouth open and drinking cool water. Also, the feathers can be held in or puffed up to act as insulation. Puffing up the feathers allows air to penetrate to the skin surface; compressing the feathers tightly creates a dead-air space for warmth. The body temperature of a Canary, 109°F, is higher than that of human beings. To keep its higher metabolism going requires much food: the average Canary weighs only two-thirds of an ounce yet eats one-eighth of an ounce of food daily, a high ratio of amount consumed to amount weighed.

DIGESTION

One very important fact about a Canary's beak is that it contains no teeth. After a few feedings, the Canary will have left many seed husks in the cage. The Canary husks the seed with its beak and swallows the grain whole. The grain passes into the throat and is held in storage in the crop. In the throat is the esophagus, and this stretches to store food. From the crop the grain passes into a glandular stomach, where it is moistened by digestive enzymes that help break it down. From the glandular stomach the seed passes into the gizzard, a muscular stomach containing gravel. The stomach muscles grind the seed against the gravel just as seed is ground up in a mill. The resulting mass passes into the intestines, where it is absorbed for nutrients. Grayish brown or black waste is later excreted.

PREENING

All birds preen, and this is a joy to behold. The bird will fluff up its feathers and shake them. It will sort through its feathers with its beak or, after flapping its wings vigorously, will pull the wing feathers through the beak to rearrange them. At the point of attachment of the long tail feathers is a small oil gland called the uropygial gland. The bird will obtain a small supply of oil from this gland and rub it on its feathers and feet as part of the preening behavior. This adds a gloss to the bird's appearance as well as protection from the elements in nature.

Color-fed Canary. Canaries can be artificially fed coloring agents that will deepen their natural color, or change their color to an orange red. These coloring agents must be administered to the bird before the onset of its moult.

7

HOLDING A CANARY

At some time your Canary may escape, so you should know how to catch and hold him. To hold your Canary, wait until his wings are in their natural position, then place your palm around his back and hold his feathers in place with your fingertips. In this way you will not risk crushing him or cutting of his breath. Nor will he be able to flap, because the pressure of your grip is over the more-sturdy wing. If you canary should escape, you should grasp him in that manner. Before trying to

A variety of seed mixtures and treats can be purchased from your local pet store. These products also come in a variety of sizes to accommodate your storage space. ◀

Border Fancy. The Border Fancy Canary does not have any of the characteristics or postures that other varieties of canaries are so difficult to breed for. ◄

Gloster Fancy Chicks. The Gloster Fancy canary is usually characterized by a crest on its head. Glosters with a crest are called "coronas" and those with the crest absent are called "consorts". ◄

catch him, make sure all fans or oven burners are turned off, and any cats or dogs removed. A tame Canary should be fairly easy to catch, though he may fly around. Move slowly and you will not alarm your pet. For a difficult to reach place you may use a perching stick rather than trying to dislodge the bird. A perching stick is a slender pole with a vertical perch attached. They can be bought at most pet stores.

TEACHING TRICKS

Birds are not known to display great intelligence, but teaching your Canary a trick or two can go right alongside taming him. Canaries have a natural fear of movement, especially over-head movement. With patience, you can teach your Canary to perch on your hand. Remove the perch and set the cage on a table until you are at eye-level with your pet. Insert a pencil or finger inside and try gently to induce the bird to perch. This usually requires some effort, and the first few tries you should coax him for no more than a few minutes. Eventually the bird should start perching on your finger and can be taught to eat seed or some treat from your finger. Pet stores sell carts and cars especially designed for birds. As the bird pecks at the seed inside, the cart moves. A Canary that can be taught to perch on your finger can be induced to eat from these toy carts.

FOOD AND FEEDING

First of all, the seed you feed your bird must be clean and fresh and

◄ In holding a canary it is important to remember to restrain the bird just enough so that it can not escape. Too much pressure exerted can harm the bird.

constant. They eat a great many times a day. The old adage of "eating like a Canary bird" should be interpreted as an insult. If humans ate as much as a Canary in proportion to their size I am sure they would soon weigh half a ton.

Dirty, dusty seed can be the source of much trouble with birds. Old seed becomes rancid, which creates more trouble. **Canary seed** is the "bread and butter" of the Canary diet. It is a bright

Red-factor Canary on hand. Canaries can be trained to perch on your hand with a lot of time and patience. ◄

White canary on hand. A canary is a nervous bird that frightens easily. While it is sitting on your hand, it would be a good idea to lightly hold the bird's feet with your thumb so that it cannot fly away. ◄

In order to train your canary to sit in the palm of your hand, you must gain the bird's trust. In order to do so, place your hand inside the cage for a few minutes each day and allow the canary to get used to it. ◄

Seed mixtures come in many varieties. To find which is the right one for your bird's needs, ask the clerk in the pet store where such products can be found. ◄

◄ Not all seeds within a mixture will be enjoyed by your bird. Birds' tastes are like human's, they will eat what they like first. It is best to try a variety of food products and then stay with the ones your bird likes best.

yellowish colored seed, rounded in the middle and pointed at the ends. It provides muscle (nitrogen), heat (carbon), phosphorus and iron for vigor as well as fibre. Its composition is: protein 13.5, fat 4.9, carbohydrates 51.6, ash 2.1, water 13.6

Rape seed is added to the Canary seed, usually about two parts Canary to one part rape seed. It is a small, brownish-black, round seed. It is rich in magnesium, lime, potash and phosphoric acid.

▶ Millet is highly enjoyed by all birds, especially canaries. Birds usually will eat only this if enough is offered. Be sure to ration such treats.

Some seed mixtures may be fed only in addition to the bird's regular diet. Products such as this can perhaps be fed only every other day. ◀

When you buy rape seed, chew up a few grains. They should be sweet and nutty tasting. If they taste bitter and biting it is not good seed. Its composition is: protein 9.4, fat 40.5, carbohydrates 10.2, ash 3.9, water 11.5

Next in importance is **grit.** When a bird eats, the food enters the crop where the grit acts as a grinding agent. Good sharp grit mixed with various minerals is good for birds. A supply should always be available in every cage. All seed companies now carry good mineral grit.

Niger seed is a shiny, elongated, almost black seed. It is an oily stimulating seed, which maintains health, enriches plumage and restores song. Its composition is: protein 17.5, fat 32.7, carbohydrates 15.3, ash 7.0, water 8.4

Poppy or **maw seed** is a small gray seed. It corrects constipation and diarrhea conditions and is readily digestible. Its composition is: protein 17.5, fat 40.3, carbohydrates 12.2, ash 5.8, water 14.6

Flax or **linseed** is a pointed reddish colored seed. This seed gives gloss to the plumage and is especially good during the moult.

There are many more supplementary seeds such as teasle, sesame, oat groats, anise, etc. All pet stores now carry good mixtures of "treat" seed which contain a mixture of these seeds. A small amount of these should be fed every day. The bird will eat what it needs of them.

A good clean piece of cuttle bone should be in every cage at all times. It furnishes minerals and vitamins and helps to keep the beak in good condition. Other food varieties may be given on different days. For instance, a piece of hard boiled egg one day, a piece of apple or orange the next day, etc.

Every bird needs some greens everyday, the darker the green the better. Kale, romaine lettuce or spinach are good greens. If you have clean dandelions in your yard there is nothing better. If you cannot obtain fresh greens there is, available in pet shops, a packaged dried green that is good. I also saw an interesting article in one pet shop. It was a little plastic dish with a greenhouse planted with seed ready to grow when water was added. I understand that new cartridges of seed are available when the first one is used up. Small flower pots can be planted with rape seed that will sprout in a few days. The flower pot can be set in the cage. The rape greens are very good food.

I have heard people say that greens give their birds diarrhea. This is because they give it just once in a while, and the bird is so hungry that it eats too much; just as a child will make himself sick on candy if given free rein. If the bird has his greens everyday he will adjust himself to the amount he needs. If your bird has not been having greens, then start with just a small amount at first.

Your local pet store carries seed mixtures that are already kept in air-tight containers. This makes it easier for you because you do not have to change the container to store it.

Yellow Border Fancy. Many natural greens are high in vitamins and nutrients. Too many greenfoods will cause loose droppings in your bird, so they should be rationed.

Border Fancy Canary. Canaries can also be fed a number of plants and greens. All of this type of food must be safe from pesticides and insecticides.

Your local pet store will supply products, such as this miniature greenhouse, so that you can sprout your own seeds. Sprouted seeds are very high in their nutritional content and are well favored by canaries. A cuttlefish-bone is a necessity in every bird's cage. Birds pick at the soft side of this for added minerals and calcium.

HOUSING

A good-sized metal cage is best for birds. They are easier to clean and do not provide the hiding places for mites that other types of cages do.

The cage should be hung about six feet from the floor in a light airy room. The airy room does not mean in a draft. There is no easier way to make a bird sick than to leave it in a draft. The temperature should be between sixty and seventy degrees as much as possible. Birds can stand extremes of heat and cold; it is sudden extreme changes that do much harm. Extreme heat makes

Canaries are very fond of bathing. A bird bath of this type can easilly be attached to the cage door. One of this design also makes it easy for you to view the bird while it is bathing. An equally delightful experience for you as well as for the bird! ◄

Canary starter kit. Your local pet store probably offers a starter package that includes everything you need to maintain your new pet in good, healthy condition. ◀

him go into a soft moult which will make him stop singing and if continued will eventually kill him. Too much tobacco fumes and gas fumes are very dangerous. Fresh paint odors can kill him in a short time.

It is natural for a bird to go to sleep soon after sundown, so if he is in a place where the lights are kept on late, at least cover his cage.

The cage should be as large as possible and the perches arranged so that the bird may exercise by flying back and forth between them.

The cage must be kept clean. If not, the bird cannot keep himself clean and dirt in his food will affect his health. The cage should be washed at intervals. The bottom of the cage should be covered with paper. Newspaper ink tends to rub

Gray Canary. Male canaries of all different colorings are very good singers, females do not sing. Pet shops carry a wide variety of colors and posture type birds from which you can choose. ◄

Bird baths are also made so that they rest upon the cage floor. Canaries prefer very cold water for their bath. Most canaries enter the bath as soon as it is placed in the cage. ◀

off on the bird and give him a dirty appearance. Pet shops have a gavel paper that can be used.

Perches should be cleaned often. There are brushes made for this purpose. If the perches are washed they should be thoroughly dried, for a damp perch will give the bird rheumatism. The perches should be oval, with cut sides. Small round perches are cruel and in time will cause much foot trouble.

The seed and water dishes should be kept clean at all times and occasionally sterilized. Just a few minutes a day does all this and really pays off with a good looking, healthy, happy bird. Only happy, healthy birds sing.

Most birds like a bath every day and will have much better looking feather texture if they have it. The water should be cool but not too cold. Different birds like different kinds of bath dishes. There is a bath dish that fits on the door of the cage. Some prefer a small tub or saucer inside. If the bird doesn't at first take a bath keep offering it, and perhaps sprinkle him a little to get him started. Experiment with your bird to find out his preferences.

A bird loves some sunlight but never, never leave him in the sun where he cannot get out of it. I have known of birds being killed by being left in too much sun with no way to escape. Never set

Variegated Canaries. Canaries are sometimes afraid of entering baths that are covered. To encourage the bird, you may place a leaf of spinach or other favorite green into the bath. ◆

◆ Frosted Canary. There have never been so many varieties of canaries to choose from as there are today. All of the different color and posture varieties are mutations from the original wild green canary.

Variegated family. The inheritance of variegated birds is such that there are always pure, unvariegated birds among the offspring.

Border Fancy. The Border Fancy Canary is a very eager and reliable breeder. If one chooses to breed canaries, the Border Fancy is the variety that one should take this hobby up with. ▲

Green Agate Canary. Agate birds are those which have   gray feathers with narrow brown edging that extends from the head to the nape, back, and wing coverts. ▼

him so the sun shines on him through glass. This can be very bad for him and his feathers. Don't hang your bird outside at the mercy of the sun, wind and stray cats. Whenever I see a bird hanging outside in a cage I am tempted to stop and tell the owner how stupid and cruel it is.

If you are so situated that you can let your bird out for a little while to fly about the room it is good for him.

When I was a child we had a Canary for a good many years. The door of his cage was never closed. He slept in it at night and visited it at intervals during the day for food, a sip of water, a bath or a short nap. My mother had an old fashioned kitchen cabinet. A shiny alarm clock was kept on the top of this. Right alongside of the alarm clock was where he spent much of his day. Whether it was the ticking of the clock that kept him company or the shiny surface where he could see himself, we could never decide. Most of his singing was done in the cage, but he had little sweet noises he made to the clock.

HEALTH CARE AND REMEDIES

If a bird is well fed, well housed and kept clean there is very little need for medicine and remedies.

If one is buying a bird they should be sure they are buying a healthy bird and then take care to keep it that way. Very often when a person realizes his bird is sick it is too late to help it. An alert, smooth feathered, bright-eyed bird that is singing is a healthy bird.

If you suspect something is wrong it is best to consult a reliable pet shop or a veterinarian who is interested in birds. They will have various tonics, antibiotics, etc., that may save your pet. If its illness has reached chronic stages don't expect them to be able to help much.

Some of the most common ailments are as follows:

Asthma—This, as with humans, affects the breathing of the bird, and can cause wheezing. It usually comes from the dust in unclean seed. In its early stage a couple of drops of iodine in the water may help. Some folks use a tiny amount of Vicks in the nostril or even in the beak. This is especially helpful if a tiny piece of seed hull has become lodged there.

Rheumatism—Usually caused by damp perches or from being left in a draft.

Diarrhea—Usually caused by wrong feeding or overfeeding of food that the bird is not in the habit of eating. A dish of poppy seed or poppy seed sprinkled on a piece of bread dipped in milk is very good for this condition.

Toenails too long—As the bird gets older, sometimes the nails grow very long and give the bird trouble holding the perch. Unless they are really bad they should be left long. In case they are bad they should be trimmed. Hold the foot up to the light. You can see the little vein running into the nail. Use nail clippers to cut the end of the nail but do not cut into the vein or the bird will bleed.

Beak too long—Occasionally the beak on an older bird grows too fast and will interfere with its cracking seed. For this condition it is wisest to consult an expert, as this is a rather delicate job and needs someone with experience.

Broken feathers—If a tail or wing feather becomes broken it should be gently pulled out. A blood vein runs into the feather and the bird can soon bleed to death if not attended to.

Scaly feet—This condition is usually caused by a tiny scale mite which gets under the scales of the feet. The feet develop hard scales and can become red and inflamed. They should be gently

Gravel paper is available at your local pet store, It is available in a variety of sizes to fit all different sized cage bottoms.

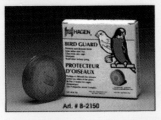

A Bird Guard is designed to hang on the side of the bird's cage to guard the bird against mite and lice infestation.

Variegated Gloster Fancy Canary. Variegated birds are characterized into groups depending upon where the variegation occurs. There are four specific areas of variegation: frontal, bridled, naped, and saddled. This bird is saddle variegated.

Breeding the Canary

Any beginner who wants to start breeding Canaries should first know something about their biology. After this he should decide on whether to breed for color or for song. To do both at the same time is impracticale. It would not be advisable to start breeding on a large scale right from the beginning, as you still lack the necessary experience.

In breeding canaries, you will most often find that the female incubates the eggs. The only time the male sits in the nest is when his mate leaves to feed. ▲

Lizard Canary with chicks. Canary chicks grow at an incredible rate. This parent bird will be kept very busy, and will appear to be constantly feeding the young. ▶

Trio of Yorkshire Canary Fledglings. Although these Yorkshire Canaries have left the nest, they have not quite completed growing. In just two months they will attain their full size. ◀

To obtain two healthy specimens requires the help of a good bird breeder or pet store owner. The mating pair should have good size for their variety and should have no defects. Experienced demonstrably fertile cocks can be bought. The purchaser should know the bird variety well before making his purchase. If you are looking for color or feather structure, you have to have an experienced eye to tell a good bird from a bad bird.

Another rule for the beginner is never to mate two yellows or two buffs together. Yellows give color and quality of feathers; buffs give size and substance of body and profusion of feathers. Mating two yellows will not necessarily give a more enhancing color or profusion of feathers. It would be better to mate a yellow with a buff to improve color and body size of a yellow.

BREEDING CAGES

Many different kinds of cages are available for breeding. A *simple cage* is used for one breeding pair. It can be constructed at home by buying a kit at your pet store or by using materials purchased at the hardware store. The simple cage is a 16" by 12" wooden frame with a wire front. The front is removable for easy cleaning. This cage usually has three perches. Two perches are placed on the back of the wooden frame so they stand vertically to the back of the cage. Another perch is placed lengthwise a few inches from the floor and stands horizontal to the viewer. Seed hoppers can be placed by the horizontal perch unless you are using an *alternate cage.*

The alternate cage is similar to the simple cage except that there are two simple cages joined by a partition. The partition is usually made out of wood for easy removal, and with a wire door so the mating pair can see each other. In this way the cock is separated from the hen until she is ready to mate, and he can still sing and feed her. For multiple matings the alternate cage is also used with three or more simple cages joined with partitions separting the birds. After fertilizing one hen, the cock can be brought to mate with other hens.

If the simple or alternate cage is hand-built, the perches should not be too thick, because this is bad for the birds' feet. The perch should be just thick enough for the bird to grasp. A nesting pan will have to be provided. This can be made of a number of different materials such as wicker, metal, or plastic, and should have holes for ventilation. A bag of nesting material can be obtained from a pet shop. It is made of soft

Canary hens sit for very long periods of time on the nest. Do not be alarmed if the female's droppings become large and odoriferous, this is normal in such situations. ◤

Canary Nest with "Dummy Eggs." Canary breeding requires a little intervention on your part. The female canary begins to incubate her eggs as soon as the first one is laid. This being so, the chicks do not all hatch on the same day, and by the time the last chick hatches, the first one is quite big. The real eggs must be removed and replaced with "dummy" eggs until the entire clutch is laid ◤

The hen canary builds her nest leaving room for her head and tail to stick out.

Canary eggs differ in coloring as they are laid. The first egg of the clutch is usually light with the remainder becoming progressively darker. The last egg is darkest in color. ◗

Variegated Canary. The way in which a variegated bird will be marked can not bo predicted nor bred for. Two symmetrically variegated birds can produce young that are not nicely marked. ◗

➤ At times during the incubation period the male may become aggressive and begin to beat up on the female. If this should happen, separate the two so that the female does not become injured.

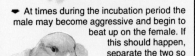

hay, moss and cowhair. When the hen is ready for mating she will begin nestbuilding. The nesting material should not be removed from in the cage too soon, as the female continues nestbuilding right up to the day she lays her first egg. She may continue nestbuilding, ripping out the nest she has already built.

In the simple cage the pair remains together during the whole breeding period. This manner of breeding has its good and bad points. Above all, the pair must show a peaceful behavior towards each other and the cock should not disturb the hen while sitting on the eggs. After the young have hatched, the cock will generally help to feed them, sometimes more actively than the female. The unfavorable points: the female proceeds to breed again sooner if the cocke remains with her, sometimes while the young are still in the nest. This forces you to provide a new nest. The female builds this up and starts to lay again. If she starts to breed, generally the fledglings still lie in the nest with her, and this may cause the eggs to be destroyed.

The *bird house* is a set-up in a room or a penthouse, males and females flying around freely in it. Their number depends on the size of the room. If you breed strains, this method is not advisable, as there is no control over which parents sire which young. In *community cages* you place one cock with three hens. This too is not advisable, as generally, major disturbances occur with this set-up.

The most economic breeding set-up, and the presently most generalized one, is the *alternate cage.* Each female is placed in a nesting cage about 16" high by 12" long and wide. One cock services 3-4 females. It is advisable to alternate the cocks for each breeding, as you cannot foresee what the singing heredity will be. Pay attention to still another point: do not permit a cock to mate with three or four females immediately. It may happen—and it often does—that he is sterile. Therefore let the cock serve one hen and wait to see whether the eggs are fertilized. Besides this, not all females are ready to lay at the same time. Thus you do not risk the danger of a whole series of females all laying infertile eggs.

GETTING THE BREEDING STOCK AND MATERIALS

It will be best to do the following: during the summer try to get acquainted with an experienced Canary breeder who owns good breeding stock. Tell him that you wish to breed Canaries. It might be advisable to join a fanciers club, where you can receive the necessary enlightenment.

The best time to purchase breeder birds is in December. The exhibitions and prize awards are over shortly after Christmas, and you may either choose the proper breeding stock yourself, or else get someone experienced to advise you. Trust an experienced fancier in this choice, as it is difficult for a beginner. New aficionados often complain: "The supplier sold me bad stock"; "The females don't feed their young, leave the eggs, etc." Suppliers cannot sell "good" or "bad" specimens, only "healthy" or "unhealthy" birds. He himself cannot predict whether the females will do their duty when breeding.

An experienced breeder, however, would never admit a failure in such things. Pay attention to the most important features to observe when buying Canary birds: a sound bird is slender and has smooth feathers. Hold the female in your hand, belly upturned, and blow the feathers on breast and belly apart. The breasts of healthy

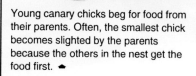

Young canary chicks beg for food from their parents. Often, the smallest chick becomes slighted by the parents because the others in the nest get the food first. ◆

Canary Fledglings. Before selling fledglings, it is important that you are sure they are consuming enough food on their own to maintain their body weight. ◆

| can place the cage in a spot where it receives sufficient light, especially sunlight, this will be very useful. Feeding the breeder hens is quite different from feeding the cocks, owing both to the large flying cage and to the low temperature. The main staple is good summer rape seed. Additionally they have to receive a varied mixed food. When to feed is your own problem. It is advisable, especially during the cold season, to serve a larger helping of the mixed food before the evening. It is also good to give some foods separate, one bowl with the rape seed, and another one with the mixed seeds. This will avoid the birds scattering food all over the cage.

Fresh water is something your birds must always have available. Except during freezing weather a daily change is sufficient. When the weather is freezing, you will have to change the water several times a day. Stop feeding greens and apples in freezing weather.

Another important point is a supplement of calcium compounds. For this, it is enough if you serve well-washed ground shells of raw eggs. Grit, too, should be amply present. If the bird's feet are caked with dirt—which happens quite frequently—soften the mud with warm water and remove it carefully. It is not infrequent that where the fancier fails to do such cleaning, inflammations may follow. You may offer your Canaries bathing water on frost-free days without fear of consequences. Females wintered in this manner will do their duty in the breeding cages. When in March the sun shines warm again, you will notice that the birds become livelier. The mating instinct awakens, and you may now start preparations for breeding.

Variegated Border Fancy. The Border Fancy is the most common breed of canary found in pet stores. This is because it is the most prolific of all canary breeds as well as a very attractive bird. ◆

Scotch Fancy. As the name lets you know, this bird originated from Scotland. This bird was very popular at the beginning of the twentieth century. Inbreeding almost destroyed the breed. Today, many breeders are striving to once again propagate the breed. ◀

THE FIRST BATCH OF FLEDGLINGS

When you start breeding, adapt to nature. If breeding is done in a heated room, it may start around the middle of March. If this is not the case, you will have to wait until the April weather is fit for it. In the former case, place the females in the breeding cages during the first days of March, and get them accustomed to the warmth gradually. Sudden changes may cause health disturbances.

After the hens have been sitting in their breeding cages for a few days, and have become used to them, you may start serving breeding food. The usual food is given as before, but you may now offer a larger proportion of egg food. Why do we feed egg food? Chicken eggs contain substances which our female Canary needs to produce her own eggs.

Give a daily helping of this food, ½ teaspoon in a special little bowl, preferably in the morning. Continue feeding rape seed and mixed food as before. Pay attention to the temperature in the nesting room when you start feeding egg food. It should be between 50-60°F.

The author serves plenty of green vegetables from the start to the end of the nesting season, with the best of success. Even if this softens the excrements a little, it is preferable to having the birds suffer from constipation. If you are lucky enough to have your breeding room face east or south, you will soon notice that the females become quite lively.

If the cocks are placed near them, and start to sing, the females will respond with loud mating calls. The mating instinct has been aroused. The hens jump around untiringly on the perches and flap their wings. Now give them nesting material which can be bought at any well-stocked pet shop. The birds pick up a beak-full, jump around

Border Fancy. Natural branches from fruit or other non-toxic trees make very good perches for canaries. The differing in diameter of the branch helps to exercise the bird's feet as well as wear down the nails. ▶

Border Fancy. Good roundness of the breast of the Border Fancy helps to make this bird a very prolific breeder. Because of the roundness, a hen Border, incubates the eggs better than a more slender breed. ▶

Japanese Hoso. Unlike the Scotch Fancy, the Japanese Hoso does not have to work to attain this posture. This slender bird assumes its posture quite naturally. ▶

Border Fancy Canary. The Border Fancy Canary is the most common breed found in pet stores. It has a very pleasant song. ➤

Gloster Fancy. The canary crest is a mutation that occurred approximately two hundred years before it was attributed as a breed in its own right.

Red-factor. This Red-factor canary has been fed artificial coloring agents. These coloring agents may be placed in the bird's food or its water.

restlessly, and carry it to the nest and back. Soon nest building begins, and the nest may be finished within a few hours.

Things that are "old hat" to the experienced breeder are not necessarily the same to the beginner. To begin with, we have to state that many a beginner places the cock in the nesting cage as soon as he puts the female there, in the hope that the cock may mate with her. There are cases in which such experiments succeed, which means that the female is already ripe for mating. Generally, however, this is not the case, and the consequence is stormy quarrels between the pair. Since she is not yet sufficiently ripe for mating, the female will simply refuse the male. The ensuing mating battles may easily lead to damages to the pair of breeders, and it may even happen that one or the other partner may lose his or her life. In order to avoid such unfortunate happenings, the cock should only be admitted near the female at the right moment, which is when she is fully ready for mating.

As a rule the Canary hen is only ripe for mating when she starts to build her nest and when her abdomen is pear-shaped, showing a reddish inflammation near the end. When the female carries building materials to the nest, sits in it, and begins to turn and shape it, this means that you should place the cock with her on the ensuing day. In most cases you will then notice that she permits the cock to fertilize her. There are cases, however, in which even a female that is ready for mating simply does not accept the cock. In this case you will have to try a ruse: admit the cock in the evening, at twilight time. Early the next morning, at dawn, turn on the light in the nesting room, and whistle a little. In most cases the female will now submit, and a red-blooded cock will bestride her, especially an experienced one. Young, untried cocks often are too clumsy for such surprise actions. If this still should fail, you will have to try another male. Should this too prove without success, exclude the female completely from the proceedings. If she lays some unfertilized eggs, let her sit on them, and give her some young from another hen to raise. Thus she will fulfill her maternal duties, and will carry out her task at the next mating. If the pair get on well with each other, without spats; if the cock does not tear down the nest; and if the hen does not wear down the cock, you may safely leave them together until the second egg is laid. Thus you avoid disturbing the birds by constantly moving them. After the first egg is laid, remove it carefully with a teaspoon and keep it in a safe place, wrapped up in cotton. The best place to keep the egg is in a flat cigar box divided into small compartments by cardboard. Each compartment is marked with the number of the nesting cage, so that you may always know the origin of the eggs. Substitute artificial eggs for the ones you remove. If you fail to do this, ensuing eggs might not be laid in the nest.

When using the simple cage it may be necessary to keep the cock in a separate cage, called a nursery, which is a small cage made of wire so the hen can still see the cock. This is one of the reasons for using the alternate cage. The male will stand by the partition and sing in an affected manner. The female displays her readiness by moving brisky every time the male sings. The female may pull feathers from her breast as an indication of nest-building. At this time it is best to put some of the nesting material in the cage; if you don't the female is likely to go right on plucking herself. The male will also bring offerings of food to the female, who will accept them through the partition. About this time the

Scotch Fancy. The Scotch Fancy does not normally stand in this position. It is trained to do so on command. A good Scotch Fancy will stand in almost a half circle position. ▸

Chopper Canary. The Chopper is a variety of song canary. Its song is wilder and more varied than that of the American Singer and the Harz Roller. ▸

◂ Scotch Fancy. The Scotch Fancy is not a bird that is normally seen in pet stores. At bird exhibitions, however, many can be seen.

Gray Canary. The slate gray coloring of this canary is often referred to as cinnamon; a very desirable color. ◆

Two Color-fed Canaries. These two birds have not been color-fed properly. The spotty appearance occurred because the birds were not fed the coloring agent prior to the onset of their moult. ◆

partition should be left open and mating should occur.

FEEDING AND HANDLING THE FLEDGLINGS

A breeder shows his real skill when handling the freshly fledged young. The young should not be weaned too soon, as they cannot eat grain if their beaks are too soft to shell it. They eat only egg food, with the consequence that they start having digestive disturbances which soon develop into intestinal diseases and eating mania. Such specimens generally cannot be cured and are lost to the fancier. You have two alternatives in order to get the birds accustomed to rape seed. You may either soak the seed in clean water or serve it shelled. Soaked rape seed has the disadvantage of easily getting covered with mildew and thus causing diseases. You will have to soak a fresh quantity for every day's feeding, and will have to remove the leftovers every night. But the birds like it a lot. Shelled rape seed is mixed with a little egg food and served this way. They never seem able to get enough of this kind of food. Offer them fresh water for drinking and bathing every day. After a few days put in some of the usual other seeds too. If the birds take and shell them, your birds will have graduated to eating grain. Beside all these seeds, also feed them some shelled oats, which should be a little shredded, and also some hemp seed. Egg food, which will have to be given during the whole summer, is now served in small quantities. Whenever possible, serve it in an elongated container, so that many birds may eat simultaneously. Egg food is best given in the morning or the afternoon.If the weather is mild, give a daily helping of greens. As was mentioned before, for this we use lettuce, spinach, the shoots of dandelions and scarlet pimpernel, the latter with as many seed pods as possible. You will notice that the birds eat the seeds first. Greens should be fed in a dry and clean state, and moderately. Nestling food, available at your pet shop, is usually very satisfactory.

The eggs from the first nesting may be put back on the third evening, as in first nestings the eggs generally number a total of four. Since it was subject to brooding for the same time, the fourth egg will hatch together with the others. On the second brooding put back four eggs, as the second laying is generally more vigorous. The number of eggs per nesting varies from 3 to 6. The last, or end egg, is recognized by its darker color. It also happens frequently, especially during the first laying, that the female skips a day between eggs. This is a natural process: eggs cannot always develop that fast.

LAYING DIFFICULTY

Laying difficulty is quite a problem. It may appear for the first egg, or for later ones. On the preceding evening the hen shows that something is wrong. She sits on her perch, with the plumage fluffed up, and breathing heavily. The next morning she can hardly reach her nest, the eyes are small, and the bird can barely keep her balance. She leaves the nest frequently, and finally sits sleeping in it or in a corner of the cage. This is the moment when you must intervene. As a start, splash some drops of cold water on her inflamed abdomen. This may revitalize the muscles of the oviduct, expelling the egg. Should the remedy fail, however, try warmth. Place the little pet in a small cage, expose it to steam for a few minutes, and then place it near a heater. This will generally bring success. Operations hardly ever succeed. It may frequently take until noon for the egg to be expelled, and you will be amazed at how quickly the Canary recovers. Frequently,

Variegated Canary. The most common variegated birds are of yellow and white coloration.

Border Fancy. The first time birdkeeper who chooses to breed his birds should begin with the Border Fancy. They are very reliable breeders as well as good parents.

Border Fancy. Although the Border Fancy is a bird with a rounded body shape, one that sits in a fluffed up position is not feeling well. Birds such as this should be medically attended to.

Red-factor. Most people who have never owned a canary are fascinated to find that they come in such an unusual color as the Red-factor.

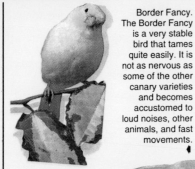

Border Fancy. The Border Fancy is a very stable bird that tames quite easily. It is not as nervous as some of the other canary varieties and becomes accustomed to loud noises, other animals, and fast movements. ◀

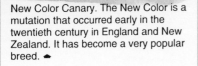

New Color Canary. The New Color is a mutation that occurred early in the twentieth century in England and New Zealand. It has become a very popular breed. ◆

White Canary. A bird that lacks all coloring in its plumage is white. White canaries are not considered albino because their eyes do not lack pigmentation. ▶

though, laying difficulty leads to death.

After the complaint is relieved, the subsequent eggs are generally sterile. This disorder is mostly caused by strong fluctuations of temperature. Furthermore it appears most frequently during the first mating. Weakened, or too fat females too, are prone to it, healthy and vigorous hens being rarely subject to this complaint.

BROODING AND HATCHING THE YOUNG

Once she sits on her eggs, the female begins to brood. During the brooding period besides rape seed she should also receive some mixed food, and every third or fourth day a pinch of egg food. If you feed only rape seed during the setting, and you suddenly give mixed food and egg food after the young have hatched, this may easily cause digestive disturbances in the females. You will often observe that the setting females turn around in the nest, or do things to the eggs with their bills. This is only natural, and need not worry you: the mother turns the eggs, which has to be done several times a day in order to have them all incubated evenly.

During the incubation period you will have to decide whether to remove the cock or not. Usually the hen will not notice if the cock is removed. However, some hens may not sit the full incubation time or may be poor mothers when the eggs hatch. Keeping the cock during incubation can be advantageous for he might sit on the eggs while the female feeds. On the other hand, he may become troublesome and break the eggs. Sometimes he will begin singing and try to lure the female away from the eggs for mating. In this case the cock should be removed. If an alternating cage is used the male will perch by the partition and sing to the female, and she may leave the eggs. So if the cock is removed he must be placed out of sight of the female. As a general rule the cock is removed; only the experienced breeder can tell what his mating pair will do. Some breeders using an alternating cage with three or more compartments will close off the brooding hen and try to get the cock to mate with another hen.

After 4-5 days of incubation you will be able to know whether the eggs are fertile or not. Take out an egg with a teaspoon and hold it up against the light. Fertile eggs are opaque, while sterile ones are clear and transparent. An experienced breeder will notice this even while the eggs are still in the nest. The best, is to wait without disturbing the female. A special "don't" is touching the eggs with your fingers and removing them from the nest. Canary eggs have a very thin and brittle shell. A teaspoon will help you to avoid mishaps!

The incubation period lasts 13 to 14 days. It may happen, however, that it extends longer, since some hen Canaries do not sit very firmly during the first days. Therefore don't be impatient and open the eggs, or, what would be worse still, try to help the young get out of their shells. This will only harm them. Young that find it difficult to leave the egg, or which cannot do this at all, are weak specimens, and will probably die anyway. After the young have hatched, check the nest for mites. The best way to check is to take out the contents and to place the nest in a hot oven for some minutes. Dry heat kills all mites. After this, let the nest cool off, and hang it back in its place. If mites suck the young intensively during the first night, you will lose them.

Don't get anxious if the female does not feed the young very much during the first days; the young still have some food in their yolk sac. If you should have the bad luck of only one or two young hatching, do not remove all other eggs

Red-factor. Red-factor canaries can be fed natural foods that will enhance their color, such as carrots or any foods that contain carotene. ←

Border Fancy with Toy. A very colorful and movable toy will catch the interest of a canary and keep it entertained for hours.

← Frosted Canary. The white edging of the feathers of a frosted canary are often referred to as scalloped or laced.

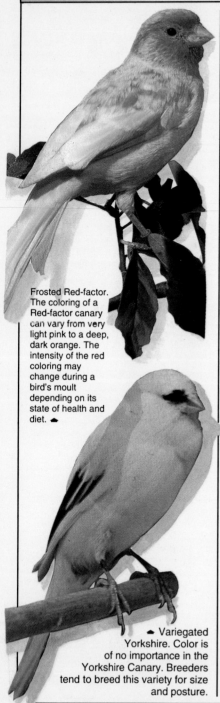

Frosted Red-factor. The coloring of a Red-factor canary can vary from very light pink to a deep, dark orange. The intensity of the red coloring may change during a bird's moult depending on its state of health and diet. ▲

▲ Variegated Yorkshire. Color is of no importance in the Yorkshire Canary. Breeders tend to breed this variety for size and posture.

immediately, but leave one or two of them in the nest. Thus the female cannot sit too heavily on the young, smothering or crippling them.

The young start growing visibly when 4-5 days old. Put the identification rings on them on the sixth to eighth day. Do not feed too much food during the first days, placing more emphasis on rape seed and mixed food. Start on the egg food after the young are some days old. The nestlings grow all their feathers by the eighteenth to twenty-first day, when they generally leave the nest. In most cases the female will now start building the nest for the next brood. If you have no substitute nest ready, clean the old one thoroughly.

The young must be at least 28 days old before they can be safely separated from the mother. If you are able to leave them with her for a few days more, this will only be of advantage. Too early weaned specimens are prone to great dangers. Therefore never be hasty!

If the female has completed her new nest in the time feeding the young allows her, don't miss the moment of putting the cock in with her again. In most cases she will accept him immediately, and laying takes place much quicker than for the first brood. Mating is not necessary after the first egg has been laid, as all eggs of the present batch are already fertilized. Pay special attention to the following: many cocks attack the young on sight and may kill them. Others feed them. Many young, too, fly on their fathers, and may disturb the mating act. The best thing to do is to remove the offspring for a short time, in order to avoid quarrels and strife. The second brooding takes place in a manner that is similar to the first one. Separate the fledglings as to sexes and place them in flying cages, after both broodings are completed.